Date: 3/21/19

OCEAN DISCOVERIES

by TAMRA B. ORR

Smithsonian is published by Capstone Press
1710 Roe Crest Drive North Mankato, Minnesota 56003
www.mycapstone.com

Library of Congress Cataloging-in-Publication Data
Names: Orr, Tamra, author.
Title: Ocean discoveries / by Tamra B. Orr. Description: North Mankato, Minn. :
Capstone Press, 2019. | Series: Smithsonian. Marvelous discoveries | Audience:
Age 7-10. Identifiers: LCCN 2018006059 (print) | LCCN 2018006749 (ebook) |
ISBN 9781543526257 (eBook PDF) | ISBN 9781543526172 (hardcover) |
ISBN 9781543526219 (pbk.) Subjects: LCSH: Ocean—Juvenile literature. |
Marine ecology—Juvenile literature. | Ocean bottom—Juvenile literature
Classification: LCC GC21.5 (ebook) | LCC GC21.5 .O77 2019 (print) |
DDC 551.46—dc23 LC record available at https://lccn.loc.gov/2018006059

Editorial Credits
Michelle Hasselius, editor; Heidi Thompson, designer;
Svetlana Zhurkin, media researcher; Kris Wilfahrt, production specialist

Our very special thanks to Don E. Wilson, Curator Emeritus, Vertebrate Zoology
at the National Museum of Natural History, for his review. Capstone would
also like to thank the following at Smithsonian Enterprises: Kealy Gordon,
Product Development Manager; Ellen Nanney, Licensing Manager;
Brigid Ferraro, Vice President, Education and Consumer Products; and
Carol LeBlanc, Senior Vice President, Education and Consumer Products.

Printed and bound in the United States
PA017

Photo Credits
© Greenpeace, 12; Alamy: Helmut Corneli, 5; Courtesy of Laura E. Bagge, 14;
Getty Images: Dante Fenolio, 23, Franco Banfi, 10; Greg Rouse, 9; MBARI: © 2006,
20, © 2009 Todd Walsh, 21 (right), © 2012, 21 (left); Minden Pictures: Solvin Zankl,
cover (bottom), 15; NASA: JPL, 29 (left), JPL/Space Science Institute, 29 (right),
JPL-Caltech, 28; Nature Picture Library: David Shale, 26; Newscom: Polaris/Tasso
Taraboulsi, 7; NOAA Ocean Explorer, 22; Scripps Institution of Oceanography at
UC San Diego: Emily Kelly, 19; Shutterstock: Alexander Kolomietz, 16, Damsea,
27, David Litman, 8, divedog, cover (top), JC Photo, 13, JonMilnes, 4, Olga
Khoroshunova, 25, Peter Hermes Furian, 6, pingebat (coral), 1 and throughout,
Russ Heinl, 17, Volina, 24 (right), Wildnerdpix, 24 (left)

Quote Sources
Page 7, "'Faceless' Fish Missing for More Than a Century Rediscovered by
Australian Scientists." 31 May 2017. The Guardian. https://www.theguardian.
com/environment/2017/may/31/faceless-fish-missing-for-more-than-a-century-
rediscovered-by-australian-scientists

Page 14, "This Ocean Creature Makes Its Own Invisibility Cloak." 9 December
2016. National Geographic. https://news.nationalgeographic.com/2016/12/
oceans-animals-invisible-physics/

Page 17, "How Drones Can Help Leopard Seals." 19 December 2017. Discover
Wildlife. http://www.discoverwildlife.com/news/how-drones-can-help-leopard-
seals

Page 29, "NASA Missions Provide New Insights into 'Ocean Worlds' in Our
Solar System." 12 April 2017. NASA. https://www.nasa.gov/press-release/nasa-
missions-provide-new-insights-into-ocean-worlds-in-our-solar-system

TABLE OF CONTENTS

DEEP IN THE SEA

Did you know there are worms shaped like Christmas trees living in the Great Barrier Reef? Have you heard of the anglerfish? It has a glowing light above its mouth. Creatures living under the ocean's surface are fascinating and mysterious—and those are just the ones scientists know about.

anglerfish

Scientists are always discovering new ocean animals. In the last 10 years, they have found 780 new kinds of crabs. They have also discovered 286 species of shrimp, as well as four sea snake species, three whale species, and three dolphin species. In total more than 226,000 species, or types, of ocean animals have been identified so far. But scientists believe there are about 1 million more species waiting to be discovered under the water.

FACELESS FISH

What fish looks like it's missing its eyes, nose, mouth, and gills? The faceless fish! In 2017 scientists from Australia spotted the fish during their expedition in the Coral Sea. The team used fishing nets and deep-sea cameras to find the fish 13,000 feet (3,962 meters) below the surface.

The faceless fish was first spotted almost 150 years ago, but it had not been seen since. Because it lives so deep in the Pacific Ocean, very few have ever been caught.

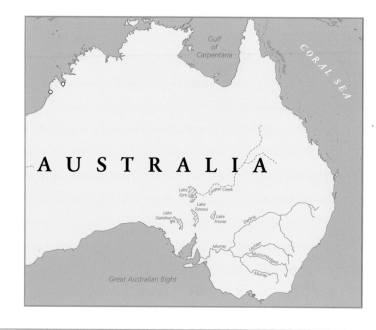

"This little fish looks amazing because the mouth is actually situated at the bottom of the animal so, when you look side-on, you can't see any eyes, you can't see any nose or gills or mouth."
—Tim O'Hara, expedition leader

CRUMPLED SOCK

The *Xenoturbella* look like a pink sock wiggling along the ocean floor. In 2016 scientists found four new species of these marine worms in the Pacific Ocean, near California and Mexico.

The worms have no organs, which make them look like crumpled-up socks or deflated balloons. They range in size from 1 to 8 inches (2.5 to 20.3 centimeters) long.

The *Xenoturbella* eat clams, oysters, and scallops.

rock scallops

Xenoturbella move so slowly that scientists had to speed up their video footage for viewers to even notice it.

A SHARK'S LIFE

The Greenland shark swims slowly in the Arctic Ocean. Scientists have known about the species since 1995. But in 2016 scientists figured out how long these sharks can live.

Greenland sharks grow about 0.5 inch (1.3 cm) per year. Adults are 13 to 16 feet (3.9 to 4.9 m) long.

Greenland sharks do not reach adulthood until they are about 150 years old.

Because the Greenland shark has soft bones, scientists can't use them to determine the animal's age. Soft bones do not show the changes that come from aging like hard bones do. Instead, forensic scientists used radiocarbon dating to determine the ages of 28 Greenland sharks. The team found that one of the sharks was 400 years old. This makes the species the longest living vertebrates on the earth.

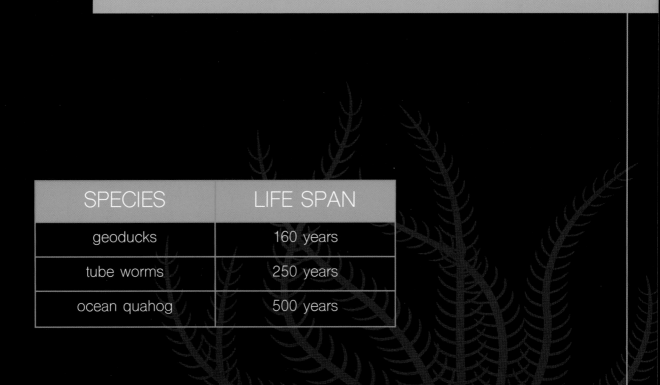

SPECIES	LIFE SPAN
geoducks	160 years
tube worms	250 years
ocean quahog	500 years

A HIDDEN CORAL REEF

It's exciting for scientists to find a new species in the ocean. Imagine finding a coral reef that's more than 600 miles (966 kilometers) long. In 2016 Brazilian and American researchers discovered the coral reef deep in the Amazon river. Most coral reefs are in shallow water to absorb the sunlight. But this reef is able to live in deeper water with limited sunlight.

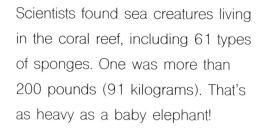

Scientists found sea creatures living in the coral reef, including 61 types of sponges. One was more than 200 pounds (91 kilograms). That's as heavy as a baby elephant!

one of the first images of the Amazon Reef, taken from a submarine in 2017

THE GREAT BARRIER REEF

The Great Barrier Reef is the planet's largest living structure. It's so large that it can be seen from outer space! It's also at risk of dying out. Warming ocean temperatures and chemicals in the water are causing the reef to die. The Australian government is taking steps to protect the Great Barrier Reef. They are limiting what can be dumped in the water and setting up funds to protect the animals living in the reef.

Divers are not able to study the coral reef up close because of strong river currents and muddy water.

NOW YOU SEE THEM, NOW YOU DON'T

If you need to hide, making yourself invisible would certainly help. Just look at the hyperiid amphipod. These sneaky crustaceans use antireflective coating to hide from hungry predators. In 2016 Laura Bagge, a marine biologist at Duke University in North Carolina, discovered that these species can seem invisible.

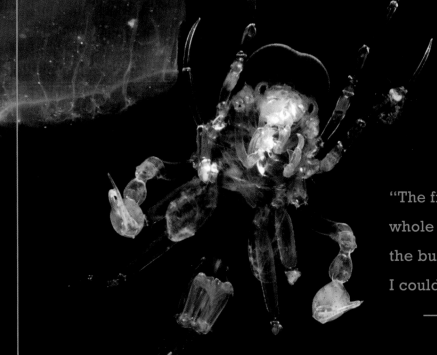

Most amphipods are not completely invisible. You can still see their colorful eyes.

"The first time we looked at what we caught, there were a whole bunch of animals in the bucket . . . I stuck my hand in the bucket . . . and instead I hit something that was hard, but I couldn't even see it . . . It looked like a glass animal."

—Laura Bagge, Duke University marine biologist

Hyperiid amphipods can grow up to 7 inches (18 cm) long. They live in almost all of the world's oceans. They are scavengers, which means they eat what they find on the ocean floors.

One of the amphipod's biggest predators are deep-sea dragon fish. Dragon fish use their own built-in lights to search for these nearly invisible creatures.

black dragon fish

KEEPING A CLOSE EYE

FROM THE SKY

Trying to track the movements and behaviors of marine animals can be difficult. They are constantly on the move, often in places that are hard—or even dangerous—for scientists to get to. That's when it's time to call in the drones. Drones can take pictures and record data quickly, without putting scientists in danger. These drones have helped with countless projects. They have recorded coral reef changes, tracked weight changes in leopard seals, and counted sea lion populations.

A hexacopter drone with a camera flies near an iceberg.

"We can get measurements that are just as good, or better, without ever bothering the animals. Catching a single seal can take hours, but the drone can photograph every seal on a beach in a few minutes."
—Douglas Krause, research scientist at the Southwest Fisheries Science Center in California

a photo of sea lions in Oregon

UNDER THE WATER

Scuba fins? Check. Mask? Check. Air tanks? Check. Microscope? Thanks to the Benthic Underwater Microscope, divers can see ocean animals up close. Researchers from Scripps Institution of Oceanography developed the microscope in 2016. Scientists can study sea creatures in their natural habitats, rather than taking them to a lab.

The Benthic Underwater Microscope has a built-in computer. It also has a ring of LED lights, a focusing lens, and can turn a photo into a 3D image.

A scientist uses the Benthic Underwater Microscope to study coral.

The microscope can go 100 feet (30.5 m) underwater. Most dive projects only go down 30 feet (9.1 m) deep.

KILLER SPONGES

Is that innocent-looking sponge in your kitchen really a dangerous killer? No, but carnivorous sponges do live deep in the oceans. These sponges often have sharp spikes to catch prey. Between 2012 and 2014, four new species of killer sponges were found in the northeastern Pacific Ocean. They were named by the Monterey Bay Aquarium Research Institute in California.

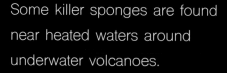

Some killer sponges are found near heated waters around underwater volcanoes.

One of these sponges is the carnivorous harp sponge. It looks like a harp. Its branches are covered in barbed hooks and sharp spines. These sponges eat zooplankton that are pushed into the branches by the ocean's current.

Scientists used remotely operated vehicles to study the sponges up close.

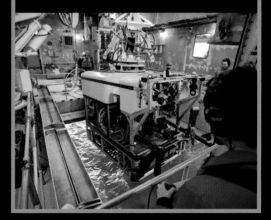

UNDERWATER DUMBO

The *Grimpoteuthis* is an octopus that has an extra set of rounded fins to propel itself through the ocean. The fins look like giant ears. Scientists call the tiny octopus Dumbo, after the character in the 1941 Disney movie, *Dumbo*.

In 2014 a team from the National Oceanic and Atmospheric Administration captured the first video of the Dumbo octopus. The animal lives on the ocean floor—9,800 to 13,000 feet (2,987 to 3,962 m) underwater. It eats snails and worms.

Most Dumbo octopuses are 8 to 12 inches (20 to 30.5 cm) long. But one octopus caught in 2009 was almost 6 feet (1.8 m) long!

Scientists have discovered more than 20 different *Grimpoteuthis* species since 1883.

UNDERWATER LANDSCAPES

Tamu Massif is the world's largest volcano, but you'll never see it up close. That's because the volcano is more than 1 mile (1.6 km) under the water. Tamu Massif was formed about 145 million years ago. It is almost 146,000 square miles. That's about the size of Japan.

Oceanographer William Sager discovered the volcano in 2013, between Japan and Hawaii. He named it "tamu" for his college, Texas A&M University.

The largest active volcano on Earth is Hawaii's Mauna Loa, but it is a fraction of the size of Tamu Massif.

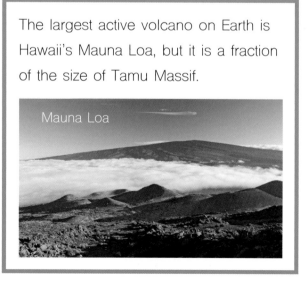

Mauna Loa

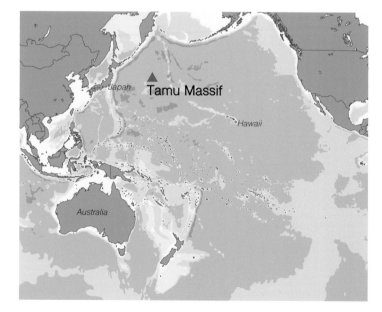

Japan   Tamu Massif   Hawaii   Australia

ALMOST A WATERFALL

An underwater waterfall flows just off the coast of Africa. Or does it? The waterfall is actually ocean currents pushing salt and silt from an underwater shelf to a much deeper one below. This fake waterfall is popular with tourists. They take helicopter rides to get a closer look.

DEEP-SEA LIZARDFISH

The deep-sea lizardfish looks like a monster from the deep. It has the face of a lizard, the body of an eel, and a mouth full of sharp, thin fangs. Luckily this fish is rarely seen. Researchers discovered the animal in the waters near Tasmania in 2017. The fishy predator lives 3,000 to 8,000 feet (914 to 2,438 m) underwater. Deep-sea lizardfish will eat anything they can find—fish, crustaceans, mollusks. They will even eat each other.

THE OCEAN'S STARS

Many oceans are home to brittle stars, or ophiuroids. Brittle stars are similar to starfish. There are hundreds of species of brittle stars that come in all colors and sizes. In 2001 a new type of brittle star was found. It can change colors in order to hide from predators.

OCEANS IN OUTER SPACE

You know that there are oceans here on Earth. But did you know there are oceans in space too? Could one of these space oceans have sea life living underwater like Earth?

In 2015 the space probe *Cassini* found hydrogen gas on one of Saturn's moons. The gas was in a large amount of icy material that sprayed up from Enceladus. Enceladus is a small moon that is covered with ice. There is a large ocean underneath the icy surface. Scientists think the gas came from the moon's ocean floor.

 ◀ *Cassini*

"This is the closest we've come, so far, to identifying a place with some of the ingredients needed for a habitable environment."

—Thomas Zurbuchen, the National Aeronautics and Space Administration (NASA)

A planet needs liquid water, a source of energy, and certain chemicals such as hydrogen, oxygen, and carbon for life to survive. Because of this discovery, scientists know that Enceladus' ocean has some of the chemicals needed to support life. Who knows if alien sea creatures are swimming in Enceladus' ocean?

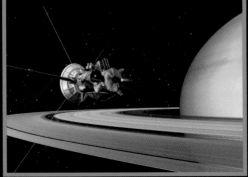

The NASA spacecraft *Cassini* was launched into space in 1997. It provided details about Saturn until 2017.

GLOSSARY

antireflective (AN-ti-ri-FLEK-tiv)—coated with a film that reduces the strength of reflected light

barb (BARB)—a hook-shaped part

carnivorous (kahr-NI-vuh-ruhss)—eating meat

coast (KOHST)—land next to an ocean or sea

crustacean (kruhss-TAY-shuhn)—a sea animal with an outer skeleton, such as a crab, lobster, or shrimp

current (KUHR-uhnt)—the movement of water in a river or an ocean

expedition (ek-spuh-DI-shuhn)—a journey with a goal, such as exploring or searching for something

fin (FIN)—a body part that fish use to swim and steer in water

forensic (fuh-REN-sik)—using science to help investigate or solve crimes

gill (GIL)—a body part on the side of a fish; fish use gills to breathe

habitat (HAB-uh-tat)—the natural place and conditions in which a plant or animal lives

marine (muh-REEN)—living in a body of water

microscope (MYE-kruh-skope)—a tool that makes very small things look large enough to be seen

mollusk (MOL-uhsk)—an animal with a soft body and no spine; a mollusk is usually protected by a hard shell

NASA (NASS-uh)—a U.S. government agency that does research on flight and space exploration

naturalist (NACH-ur-uhl-ist)—a scientist who studies animals and plants

radiocarbon dating (ray-dee-oh-KAR-buhn DAYT-ing)—a method of measuring the type of carbon in an object to determine how old it is

scavenger (SKAV-uhn-jer)—an animal that feeds on whatever it can find

silt (SILT)—small particles of soil that settle at the bottom of a river, lake, or ocean

vertebrate (VUR-tuh-brit)—any animal that has a backbone; fish are vertebrates

volcano (vol-KAY-noh)—an opening in the earth's surface that may send out hot lava, steam, and ash

zooplankton (ZOO-plangk-tuhn)—small floating or weakly swimming organisms that drift with water currents

CRITICAL THINKING QUESTIONS

1. Hyperiid amphipods are scavengers. What does "scavenger" mean? Name another animal that is a scavenger.

2. Harp sponges are carnivores. Name another carnivorous sponge.

3. Explain the differences between brittle stars and starfish.

READ MORE

Mason, Paul. *World's Weirdest Sharks*. Wild World of Sharks. Minneapolis: Hungry Tomato, 2018.

Rake, Jody S. *Kings of the Oceans*. Animal Rulers. North Mankato, Minn.: Capstone Press, 2018.

Simon, Seymour. *Sea Creatures*. New York: HarperCollins, 2018.

INTERNET SITES

Use FactHound to find Internet sites related to this book.

Visit *www.facthound.com*

Just type in 9781543526172 and go.

Check out projects, games and lots more at
www.capstonekids.com

INDEX